more
Words of Love
A Collection of Quotes
About Love

Created By

Ian Wilson

ISBN: 9781507605080

Printed in U.S.A

www.wordsoflove.ca

Contents

Introduction

Page

Introduction

Here in the second part of my collection of quotes of love, I have divided them into four chapters.

In chapter one are, quotes about old and new love. In this section people express from their mind and spirit how they feel when love has crossed their path.

Chapter two has quotes about marriage and relationships. For a relationship to survive in today's world, a couple must learn to compromise, keep communication lines open and forgive quickly.

Hard hearts will only break a relationship. Soft hearts are teachable and will survive the storms. Saint Augustine said, "Bitterness imprisons life, love releases it."

Chapter three has quotes about showing affection. A kiss in the morning can change your aura for the rest of the day.

Having a loved ones' arms around you, generates feelings of love, warmth and comfort. Feelings of despair and misery dissipate.

When we show affection for one another, it shows that we care deeply about each other and that we are not afraid to let others see.

Chapter four contains sad love quotes.
Life can be empty when we can't find that special soul to complete our life with or when a loved one departs.
A heavy and torn heart can be accompanied by many days and nights of a void, barren and doleful life.
Tender words can help sooth our hearts and help them to mend.
We must never lose hope in finding love.
Lots of love is out there; it is just a matter of time before we will find love again

Chapter 1

Love Old and New

When you love a woman, you see your world inside her eyes.

I chose to love you in silence, for in silence I find no rejection. I chose to love you in your loneliness, for in your loneliness no one owns you, but me.

The love you have given me has made days brighter. The thought of losing you will be the end of me, so let me love you till our hearts stop beating.

You are the gold thread running through the warm blanket of my life.

He looks at me and my heart starts skipping beats, my face starts to glow, and my eyes start to twinkle. Imagine what he would do to me if he smiled.

A great lover is not one who loves many, but one who loves one woman for life.

An angel isn't heaven sent, but is the person sitting next to you serving as your motivation to live for their love.

Love is a perfume you cannot pour onto others without getting a few drops on yourself.

A woman's love is a man's privilege, not his right.

Lust is a state of the mind; love is a state of the heart and soul.

The world is a puzzle and we're two pieces that fit perfectly together.

My thoughts are free to go anywhere, but it's surprising how often they head in your direction.

I'm looking for the man who will ruin my lipstick, not my mascara.

Choosing a love and then being strong enough to live up to your commitment of love is the essence of love.

I begin to speak and he can finish my sentence; he looks into my eyes and speaks my thoughts, for two have become one.

They say you only fall in love once but every time I look at you, I fall in love all over again.

Sacred and sweet was all I saw in her.

William Shakespeare

You attract people by the qualities you
display. You keep them by the qualities you
possess.

You know you're really in love, when you
have love for that person and only that person.

You want to be with them in every waking
moment, and you'll stay with them through
thick and thin.

So, fall asleep love, loved by me.
For I know love, I am loved by thee.
Paradise is always where love dwells.

Richter

A guy who loves his girl doesn't need to unbutton her shirt to get a better view of her heart.

Love is reaching for someone's hand, and holding their heart.

I like not only to be loved, but to be told I am loved.

You know it is love when you want to keep holding hands even after they are sweaty.

One word frees us of all the weight and pain in life. That word is love.

In myself I know I have everything. In you I know I obtained meaning.

I should tell you how I really feel, but I'm afraid of what you might say.

I cheated on my fears and
broke up with my doubts.
I got engaged to my Faith,
now I'm marrying my Dreams.
Soon I will be holding hands with
my Destiny!

I'll follow you and make a heaven out of hell
and I'll die by your hand which I love so well.

William Shakespeare

Insanity and love are very much alike.
You're crazy in both states.

I worry when you miss me, but it hurts when you don't.

Love isn't blind. It just isn't looking your way at the moment.

You don't love a girl because of beauty. You love her because she sings a song only you can understand.

Sometimes someone says something really small and it fits right into this empty place in your heart.

Since we can't be together for the moment, meet me in your dreams.

My love for you can't be contained because my heart loves you way beyond its fullest capacity.

Me being with any other girl is just settling for less.

Where my head rests is not where my thoughts lay.
Wish chastely, and love dearly.

William Shakespeare

My love; when I'm in your arms, it's like the whole world doesn't exist.

Love is friendship set on fire.

French Proverb

A great lover is not one who loves many, but one who loves one woman for life.

I never really understood the term better half' until I met her.

When you love someone, telling them you love them isn't enough.
You must make them feel the love that you have for them.

Love me when I least deserve it, because that's when I need it most.

The world without love would be like a garden without flowers, and life without love would be more tortuous and less humane.

Dr T.P. Chia

Today is another day whereby our love can grow even more.

When I'm alone, I think of so many things to say to you, but when I have a chance to tell you, I go speechless.

True love is unconditional and everlasting; it is established over time and validated with memories of the past.

True love is distinguished by what it offers, not by what it demands.

First love is when your lips smile, but true love is when your heart laughs all the time.

You know you're in love when at those times, you're apart, you find yourself gazing at the sky in the direction she lives and feeling some peace in knowing that you live under the same sky.

If you were to measure the fire of our love, it would put hell to shame.

Happiness is falling asleep next to you and waking up thinking I'm still in my dreams.

I pretended to look around, but I was looking at you.

Whenever you see love coming, welcome it with open arms and let it enter you.

People will ask, 'Are you in love?' You will say, 'No, love is in me.'

Love is when you don't have to be with another person to touch their heart.

Heaven's harmony is universal love.

Cowper

Falling in love with someone isn't always going to be easy. It is often filled with anger and tears. It is when you want to be together despite it all. That is when you are truly in love.

When you can see your unborn children in her arms, you know you really love a woman.

Love is the sweetest of dreams, and the worst of nightmares.

Love is like standing in wet cement.
The longer you stay, the harder it is to leave.

Infatuation and intimacy ignites love;
commitment makes the flame keep on
burning.

I could do without many things with no
hardship; you are not one of them.

Ashleigh Brilliant

Love is not a matter of counting the years, but
making the years' count.

Look into my eyes and you'll see what your
love is doing to me.
My eyes have learned to smile.

Love is like a card game; sometimes you're dealt a good hand; sometimes you have to work with what you've got, and sometimes you have to fold, and hope the next hand dealt is playable.

Love is being awakened by a kiss.

The mind makes the love start, but the heart makes the love grow.

I may not hear every word you speak, but the sound of your voice is music to my ears.

Never me without thee, nor thee without me.
I am a rose; you are my thorns, clutching and
protecting me.

Upon thy cheek, I lay this zealous kiss, as seal
to the indenture of my love.

William Shakespeare

Is not every true lover a martyr?

Hare

Heaven may be hidden in the clouds, but I see
it every day, just by being with you.

Just thinking about you makes me smile.
He said, "I like when it does though."

Love can sun the realms of night.

Schiller

When Eternity comes I'll still be at your side.

I don't want to be your whole life, just your favorite part.

To love someone is giving them your heart
but trusting them not to break it.

Every time we talk, I fall a little harder.

The head learns new things, but the heart
forever practices old experiences.

Take away love and our earth is a tomb.

Robert Browning

Love is when you wake up thinking of no one else, but that person.

Husbands are like fine wine.
They take time to mature.

Love is the egotism of two.

Love is like a shoe; it cushions your walk through life.

Love is but a seed in your heart, with care it will blossom into a beautiful flower.

Successful love takes a load off our hearts, and puts it upon our shoulders.

Bovee

Man loves little and often, woman much and rarely.

Basta

Honest men love women; those who deceive them adore them.

When asked where's heaven, I pointed at you and said, "in his arms." So, when you wonder why I always say I would love to die in your arms, it's because I know I'll end up in heaven.

Love, which is only an episode in the life of man, is the entire history of woman's life.

Madame de Staël.

In her first passion, woman loves her lover; in all the others, all she loves is love.

My soul hath her content so absolute that not another comfort like to this succeeds in unknown fate.

William Shakespeare

The fountain of love is the rose and the lily,
the sun and the dove.

Heinrich Heine

What a miserable world; trouble if we love,
and trouble if we do not love.

The most precious possession that ever comes
to a man in this world is a woman's heart.

J.G. Holland

Love's gentle spring doth always fresh
remain.

William Shakespeare

Riches take wings, comforts vanish, hope
withers away, but love stays with us.
Love is God.

A flower cannot blossom without sunshine,
and a man cannot live without love.

The sweetest joy, the wildest woe is love.
What light on yon window breaks?
'Tis the east, and Juliet is the sun."

William Shakespeare, Romeo and Juliet

Only those who love with the heart can
animate the love of others.

Bitterness imprisons life, love releases it. Love is the beauty of the soul.

Saint Augustine

Love is either the disease that kills you or the vaccine that keeps you alive!

A home without a mate is just a pile of cold bricks.

If kissing was just two people touching lips, it wouldn't touch our hearts and bind our souls the way it does.

So, fall asleep love, loved by me, for I know
love, I am loved by thee.
See, how she leans her cheek upon her hand!
O, that I were a glove upon that hand, that
I might touch that cheek!

William Shakespeare

In myself I know I have everything.
In you I know I obtained meaning.

Never me without thee, nor thee without me.

Love is a potent emotion. It affects the
physical and mental state of wellbeing.

What if I fall? Oh, but my darling,
What if you fly?

You make me happy, you make me laugh.
Your smart, your different.
You're a little crazy and awkward and your
smile alone can make my day.

I want a new life and I want it with you.
Wouldn't it be the perfect crime,
If I stole your heart and you stole mine?

When you trip over love, it is easy to get up.
But when you fall in love, it is impossible to
stand again.

Albert Einstein

You are the finest, loveliest, most tender, and most beautiful person I have ever known. Even that is an understatement.

F. Scott Fitzgerald

Yes, I am crazy because of you? The truth? I like you a lot.

I fell in love with the way you fall asleep, slowly and then all at once.

Bitterness imprisons life, love releases it. Love is the beauty of the soul.

Saint Augustine

You can't force someone to love you
You can only stalk them and hope for the
best.

Art, thou not dearer to my eyes than light?
Dost, thou not circulate through all my veins?
Mingle with life, and form my very soul?

There is no more delightful hour in life
than that of an unconfessed but mutual love.

Love is an egotism of two.

Antoine de Salle.

My angel flew out of my dream and into my arms.

Inhaling your breath into my body, taking you into my soul, all this, through a kiss.

Mutual love, the crown of all our bliss.

Milton.

If you stood in front of a mirror holding 11 roses; you will see 12 of the most beautiful things in this word.

You are charged with stealing my heart trespassing in my dreams and robbing me of my senses
Your sentence is, life with me.
How do you plead?

Love that has nothing but beauty to keep it in good health, is short-lived.

I fell in love with the way you touched me without using your hands.

I never thought love was worth fighting for, but then I looked into your eyes and I am ready for war.

No cord or cable can draw so forcibly, or bind so fast, as love can do with only a single thread.

I look at you and see the rest of my life in front of my eyes.

My love to you is everlasting; it will never grow old and it will never fade away.
I will forever love you.

Never be jealous again. Never doubt that
I love you more than the world.
More than myself.

Camille

Somewhere there's someone who dreams of
your smile, and finds in your presence that
life is worthwhile.

No cord or cable can draw so forcibly, or bind
so fast, as love can do with only a single
thread.

Chapter 2

Marriage and Relationships

Sex isn't special unless it is shared inside the boundaries of marriage, and then, 'sex' is not a deep enough word to describe it. For then, it's 'making love' and making love is the greatest gift in the world. True love waits.

.

Because you have my heart, I am asking for your hand.

A marriage is not a 50/50 compromise
It takes both husband and wife giving
100/100.

Love is like a friendship caught on fire.
In the beginning a flame, very pretty, often
hot and fierce, but still only light and
flickering. As love grows older, our hearts
mature and our love becomes as coals,
deep-burning and unquenchable.

Bruce Lee

I can never be the perfect wife, but I'm willing
to be perfect for you

Someday, you will find the one who will
watch every sunrise with you until the sunset
of your life.

Where's home for you? a stranger asked a
fellow traveler. "Wherever she is, he replied,
as he pointed at his wife."

When you realize, you want to spend the rest
of your life with somebody, you want the rest
of your life to start as soon as possible.

When Harry Met Sally

Distance can accelerate a corrupt relationship
down in flames but it can make a worthy
relationship resistant to fire.

I want a new life and I want it with you.

Missing you is my hobby, caring for you is my job, making you happy is my duty, and loving you is my life.

Don't marry a person you can live with; marry somebody you can't live without.

Marriage is a forever thing; you should love your partner this day and forever.

You should tell your soul mate everything. Don't hide anything because if it's true love they'll understand and be there for you.

It is a constant appreciation for each other
and a thoughtful demonstration of gratitude.
It is encouraging and helping each other
to grow.
Marriage is a joint quest for the good, the
beautiful and the divine.

James E. Faust

No woman should marry until she has studied
anatomy and dissected at least one man.

My husband and I have never considered
divorce... murder sometimes, but never
divorce.

Joyce Brothers

When you love someone, you love the whole person, just as he or she is, and not as you would like them to be.

William Shakespeare

Woman came from man's rib.
Not from his feet to be walked on.
Not from his head to be superior.
But from his side to be equal, under his arm to be protected and close to his heart to be loved.

Love is taking two hearts and blending them into one.

I love being married. It's so great to find that one special person you want to annoy for the rest of your life.

Rita Rudner

My heart is entwined around yours forever and ever.

What greater thing is there for two human souls, than to feel that they are joined for life to strength each other in all labor, to rest on each other in all sorrow, to minister to each other in silent unspeakable memories at the moment of the last parting?

George Eliot

Doubt thou the stars are fire.
Doubt that the sun doth move.
Doubt truth to be a liar.
But never doubt I love you.

William Shakespeare
Hamlet

You'll know when a relationship is right for you.
It will enhance your life, not complicate your life.

Missing someone is your hearts way of reminding you that you love them.

The heart has its reasons which reason knows not.

Blaise Pascal

A happy marriage is a long conversation which always seems too short.

Andre Marois

The best love is the kind that awakens the soul and makes us reach for more, that plants a fire in our hearts and brings peace to our minds.

Nicholas Sparks, The Notebook

To keep your marriage brimming, with love in the loving cup, whenever you're wrong admit it, whenever you're right shut up.

If I get married, I want to be very married.

Audrey Hepburn

You may hold my hand for a while, but you hold my heart forever

If you're asking if I need you, the answer is forever. If you're asking if I will leave you, the answer is never. If you're asking what I value, the answer is you. If you're asking if I love you, the answer is I do

Don't smother each other. No one can grow in the shade.

Leo F. Buscaglia

My love for you is a journey starting at forever and ending at never.

The best thing a father can do to his children is love their mother.

All the little things you do warm my heart.
You are a constant source of joy in my life.
You are forever and always the hero of my
heart, the love of my life.

When we get to the end of our lives together,
the house we had, the cars we drove, the
things we possessed won't matter.
What will matter is that I had you and you
had me.

I am forever grateful for the happiness and
joy you have brought into my life.

A successful marriage requires falling in love
many times, always with the same person.

Mignon McLaughlin

I love you neither with my heart, nor with my mind. My heart might stop; my mind can forget. I love you with my soul because my soul never stops or forgets.

Rumi

I want to hold your hand at 80 and say we made it.

I wish I could turn back the clock, I'd find you sooner and love you longer.

My friend, when you love, let it be a woman whom you can love forever.

Some people ask the secret of our long
marriage. We take time to go to a restaurant
two times a week. A little candlelight, dinner,
soft music and dancing.
She goes on Tuesdays, I go Fridays.

Henry Youngman

We're truly not apart.
Until the final breath I take, you'll
be living in my heart.

Assumptions are the termites of relationships.

Henry Winkler

Success in marriage does not come merely
through finding the right mate, but through
being the right mate.

Marriage is like watching the color of leaves in the fall; ever changing and more stunningly beautiful with each passing day.

Fawn Weaver

Never love anybody that treats you like you're ordinary.

Oscar Wilde

Marriage is like a phone call in the night: first the ring, and then you wake up.

Evelyn Hendrickson

A lovers' quarrel is always about every quarrel you ever had.

Robert Brault

The greatest marriages are built on teamwork, mutual respect, a healthy dose of admiration, and a never-ending portion of love and grace.

Fawn Weaver

In marriage, each partner is to be an encourager rather than a critic, a forgiver rather than a collector of hurts, an enabler rather than a reformer.

When you don't talk, there's a lot of stuff that ends up not getting said.

Catherine Gilbert Murdock

What counts in making a happy marriage is not so much how compatible you are, but how you deal with incompatibility.

Leo Tolstoy

Hold no grudges and practice forgiveness. This is the key to having peace in all your relationships.

Wayne Dyer

The real act of marriage takes place in the heart, not in the ballroom or church or synagogue. It's a choice you make on your wedding day and forever.
It is reflected in the way you treat your husband.

Barbara De Angeli

Marriages, like a garden, take time to grow.
But the harvest is rich unto those who
patiently and tenderly care for the ground.
The beauty of marriage is not always seen
from the very beginning but rather as love
grows and develops over time.

Fawn Weaver

I have lived long enough to know that the
evening glow of love has its own riches and
splendor.

Benjamin Disraeli 1804 – 1881

Marriage is not a ritual or an end.
It is a long, intricate, intimate dance together
and nothing matters more than your own
sense of balance and your choice of partner.

Amy Bloom

Secrets are festering parasites to a relationship, devouring their hosts from within, leaving behind an empty hollow husk of what once was.

Mark W. Boyer

The more you invest in a marriage, the more valuable it becomes.

Amy Grant

There is no pain equal to that which two lovers can inflict on one another.

Cyril Connolly

Never let a problem to be solved become more important than a person to be loved.

Barbara Johnson

In the enriching of marriage, the big things
are the little things. There must be constant
appreciation for each other and thoughtful
demonstration of gratitude. A couple must
encourage and help each other grow.
Marriage is a joint quest for the good,
the beautiful, and the divine.

James E. Faust

Marriage is not the ritual or an end, it is a
long, intricate, intimate dance together and
nothing matters more than your own sense of
balance and choice of partner.

Amy Bloom 1953

In marriage, do thou be wise: prefer the
person before money, virtue before beauty,
the mind before the body; then thou hast a
wife, a friend, a companion, a second self.

William Penn

Every couple needs to argue now and then. Just to prove that the relationship is strong enough to survive. Long-term relationships, the ones that matter, are all about weathering the peaks and the valleys.

Nicholas Sparks

Just because a relationship ends, it doesn't mean it's not worth having.

Sarah Mlynowski

The goal in marriage is not to think alike, but to think together.

If a relationship is to evolve, it must go through a series of endings.

She who dwells with me whom I have loved
with such communion, that no place on Earth
can ever be solitude to me.

William Blake 1770 - 1850

.

Where we love, is home.
Home that our feet may leave, but not our
hearts.

Oliver Wendell

Marriage is not a static state between two
unchanging people. Marriage is a
psychological and spiritual journey that
begins in the ecstasy of attraction, meanders
through a rocky stretch of self-discovery, and
culminates in the creation of an intimate,
joyful, lifelong union.

Harville Hendrix

Well, what is a relationship?
It's about two people having tremendous
weaknesses and vulnerabilities, like we all do,
and one person being able to strengthen the
other in their areas of vulnerability, and vice
versa. You need each other.
You complete each other, passion and
romance aside.

Jane Fonda

Let the wife make the husband glad to come
home, and let him make her sorry to see him
leave.

Martin Luther

There is nothing nobler or more admirable
than when two people, who see eye to eye,
keep house as man and wife, confounding
their enemies and delighting their friends.

Homor

Love is the most ecstatic intensive consciousness of the cosmic forces of the universe.

What cosmic currents can pass through the holding of hands and communion of bodies of two beings in love!

Robert Muller

Our wedding was many years ago,
The celebration continues to this day.

A good marriage is that in which each appoints the other, guardian of his Soul.

Rainer Rilke

Thou art my life, my love, my heart.

Married couples who love each other, tell each other a thousand things, without talking.

Two things doth prolong thy life, a quiet heart and a loving wife.

Problems are not stop signs, they are guidelines.

Robert H. Schuller

Let there be spaces in your togetherness.

Be presidents of each other's fan clubs.

Tony Heath

As for his secret to staying married:
my wife tells me that if I ever
decide to leave, she is coming with me.

Jon Bon Jovi

Marriage is three parts love and seven parts
forgiveness of sins.

 Lao Tzu

A simple enough pleasure, surely, to have
breakfast alone with one's husband, but how
seldom married people in the midst of life
achieve it.

Anne Morrow Lindbergh

To get divorced because love has died,
is like selling your car
because it's run out of gas.

Whenever you're in conflict, there is one
factor that can make the difference between
damaging your relationship and deepening it.
That factor is attitude.

William James

One of the hardest parts of life is deciding
whether to walk away or try harder.

Love is caring for each other even when you
are angry.

I'd rather have bad times with you, than good times with someone else.
I'd rather be beside you in a storm, than safe and warm by myself.
I'd rather have hard times together, than to have it easy apart.
I'd rather have the one who holds my heart.

Let there be spaces in your togetherness.
From the first moment, I saw you I knew that I wanted to be with you forever. I'm so glad to be celebrating our first anniversary with you.

Because you have my heart, I am asking for your hand.

Chapter 3

Showing Affection

If you give me your kiss for breakfast, your
hug for lunch and your love for dinner,
I promise you will never catch me eating
elsewhere, because I have no reason to do so.

Kissing is a merging of two lips, two souls
and two spirits that makes them divine.

You're like a teddy bear; easy to love, easy to
hold

I'll give you an ocean of love, with a kiss on every wave.

Being held in your arms for only a few seconds takes all the pain of the world away from me.

Can I borrow a kiss? I promise to give it right back!

Simple music can make you sing, a simple hug can make you feel better, simple things can make you happy; I hope my simple hello will make you smile.

If I reach for your hand, will you hold it?
If I hold out my arms, will you hug me?
If I go for you lips, will you kiss me?
If I capture your heart, will you love me?

If you like me you'll let me know, but if you
hug me you let it show.

Lips that endorsed your breath, sealed with a
righteous kiss.

William Shakespeare

A hug is like a bandage to a hurting wound.

The world would be a better place if we smiled more often and hugged a bit longer. If only I was with you, I would kiss you. If only was beside you, I would embrace you tight. But since I'm far from you, I'll let the angels do it for me today ... but next time it will be my turn.

The more hugs you give or receive, the happier you are and the longer you live!

There is nothing that feels as good as you wrapped inside my arms.

Affection is the kind of love that leaves you feeling close, safe, and cared for.

A hug for you means I need you. A kiss for you means I love you. A call for you means I'm missing you.

A hug overcomes all boundaries. It speaks words within the mind that cannot be spoken.

There are moments in life when you miss someone so much that you just want to pick them from your dreams and hug them for real.

A hot guy opens my eyes, a smart guy opens my mind, but only a sweet guy can open my heart.

When you came, you were like red wine and honey, and the taste of you burnt my mouth with its sweetness.

Hershey makes a million kisses a day, I'm just asking for one.

Hug and kiss her and tell her you love her in bed before you both go to sleep.

Jealousy is the grave of affection.

My affection hath an unknown bottom, like the Bay of Portugal.

Don't let a fool kiss you, and don't let a kiss fool you.

A kiss without a hug is like a flower without the fragrance.

Trust in my affection for you.

Giving lots of affection and getting none in return hurts more than you think.
Never leave a true relationship for a few faults.
Nobody is perfect, nobody is correct.
In the end affection is always greater than perfection.

If you love her:
Help her clear off the table and wash and dry the dishes with her, giving her a hug and kiss at least once, and tell her that you love her.

I was not kissing him. I was just telling his lips a secret!

There's nothing sexier than a man who is in love with his woman and is not afraid to show it.

Care doesn't need powerful eyes or a cute voice or a lovely face. It always needs a beautiful, responsible heart with affection forever.

If equal affection cannot be, let the more loving be me.

If you love her:
Buy her flowers on the way home at least once a week, with a card that tells her you love her.

In nine cases out of ten, a woman had better show more affection than she feels.

Jane Austen

Do you know what it means to come home at night to a woman who'll give you a little love, a little affection, a little tenderness?
It means you're in the wrong house, that's what it means.

Henry Youngman

Three A's to keep your girl: affection, adoration and attention. Three C's to keep a relationship: communication, commitment and care.

Sometimes we let affection, go unspoken.
Sometimes we let our love go unexpressed.
Sometimes we can't find words to tell our feelings.
Especially towards those we love the best.

Sometimes all you need is a hug from the right person, and all your stress will melt away.

We all know him to be a proud, unpleasant sort of man; but this would be nothing if you really liked him.

Jane Austen, Pride and Prejudice

To make a woman happy, give her these three things. Attention, affection and appreciation. I was born with an enormous need for affection, and a terrible need to give it.

Audrey Hepburn quotes

Sometimes I just want a hug. Sometimes I want to feel wanted, I want affection. Sometimes I just want to hear your voice and know that you care.

We fear rejection, want attention, crave affection and dream of perfection.

Just because you have a guy's attention doesn't mean you have his affection.

Affection is responsible for nine-tenths of whatever
solid and durable happiness there is in our lives.

C. S. Lewis

The affections are like lightning: you
cannot tell where they will strike till they
have fallen.
Don't be afraid of showing affection.
Be warm and tender, thoughtful and
affectionate. Men are more helped by
sympathy than by service.
Love is more than money, and a kind
word will give more pleasure than a
present.

Sir John Lubbock

If you love her:
Call her during the day to ask how she is
doing and that you love her.

The best way to hold a man is in your arms.

If equal affection cannot be,
When you give her affection, she believes
that you love her and care about her problems.
Your affectionate touch, actions and words
open the door to her heart and allow her to
respond to you with passion.

Everything in the world is so fine, but
everything is not mine.
There is one thing that is so divine, it is
your love and luckily, it's mine.

Let the more loving one be me.

W.H. Auden

If you love her:
Tell her that you love her while you are
having breakfast together.

Affection takes the loving relationship between a man and woman in marriage into the deeper realm of tender expressions. It's one that results in feelings of closeness, passion, and security.

Love is not to be purchased, and affection has no price.

St. Jerome

The marriages most likely to end in divorce are those where expressions of affection and love are lacking.

Affection isn't time, but it requires time to accomplish.
Affection isn't communication. But without communication, there can be no affection.
Affection isn't romance, but it typically involves romantic spontaneity, creativity, and fun.

Most people would rather give than get affection.

Aristotle

If somebody likes me, I want them to like the real me, not what they think I am.
I don't want them to carry it around inside.
I want them to show me, so I can feel it too.

If you love her:
Kiss her and tell her you love her before
you leave for work.

Take me on a date to a coffee shop.
Show me wild affection, make me shy,
tell me comments to make me nervous.

Love is what makes two people sit in the
middle of a bench when there is plenty of
room at both ends

Affection is responsible for nine-tenths of
whatever solid and durable happiness there
is in our lives.

C.S. Lewis

The hardest of all is learning to be a well of affection, and not a fountain, to show them that we love them, not when we feel like it, but when they do.

Trust in my affection for you.

One must not be mean with the affections; what is spent of the fund is renewed in the spending itself.

Sigmund Freud

Affection reproaches, but does not denounce.

A woman's whole life is a history of the affections.
The heart is her world: it is there her ambition strives for empire; it is there her avarice seeks for hidden treasures.
She sends forth her sympathies on adventure. She embarks her whole soul on the traffic of affection; and if shipwrecked, her case is hopeless, for it is a bankruptcy of the heart.

If you catch me looking at your lips when you talk, just kiss me.

Deep is a wounded heart, and strong.
A voice that cries against a mighty wrong.
And full of death as a hot wind's blight,
Doth the ire of a crushed affection light.

Felicia Hermans

I literally crave affection. It's not about sex.
I crave somebody to cuddle me and to lay
their head on my lap.
I crave kisses, holding hands and running my
thumb across theirs.
Just looking at someone and thinking,
"how did I get this lucky".

That trial is not fair where affection is judge.

Yes, I do touch. I believe that everyone
needs that.

Princess of Wales Diana

Sometimes I'm scared that I'll
open my mouth and all my unfiltered
feelings will come gushing out.
What if you hear me?
What if you don't?

I just want to hold you and stare into your
eyes.
We don't have to talk, I just want to
appreciate your existence.
I need to kiss you so badly.
One of those kisses where I'm pressing
against you as much as possible and my hands
are in your hair and moving down your back.
Clutching you in any way I can, kissing you
as deeply as possible and thinking you're
mine, mine. mine.

The slower the kiss, the faster the heartbeat.

The way to love someone is to lightly run
your finger over that person's soul until you
find a crack, and then gently pour your love
into that crack.

I crave your arms around me. I crave the sound of your voice in my ears; your laugh the most. I crave your smile that lights up your face. I crave your presence by my side.

I crave affection but also run from it.

If you like someone, you wish them well.
But.
If you love someone, you breathe wellness into them.

Sima Mittal

Why is it that
Every time I sit down and relax
My mind wanders to you?
Not that I mind, I suppose
It's nice to think about what could
happen between us, such as touching,
kissing.
If I only had the courage.

Even with friends, I had difficulty giving or receiving physical affection, although I secretly craved it.

I'm telling you this for one reason and one reason only: No matter how sure you are of someone's love, it's always nice to hear it.

It's true that nothing in this world makes us so attached to others as the affection we have for them.

It was a lesson most people learned much earlier; that even friendship could have an undisclosed shelf life.
That loyalty and affection, so consuming and powerful, could dissipate like fog.

Jennifer Haigh, The Condition

A concrete love is a mass of emotion formed into a compound mixture of affection, care, desire and expectation.

Munia Khan

Affection is like bread, unnoticed till we starve, and then we dream of it, and sing of it, and paint it.

Emily Dickinson

She rested her head against his and felt for the first time, what she would often feel with him: a self-affection.
He made her like herself. With him, she was at ease; her skin felt as though it was her right size.

Lily King

I felt sad.
I felt cold.
I felt hurt.
I felt forsaken and lonely.
I felt doubtful and hesitant.
I felt scared and deeply worried.
I felt different, unknown, and unwelcome.
I felt empty and woefully neglected.
I felt weak and intimidated.
I felt withdrawn and shy.
I felt utterly hopeless.
Then you held my hand,
and I felt better.

Richelle E. Goodrich, Slaying Dragons

Passion lingers on a state of bliss
Love loves you more when you kiss.

It is the passion that is in a kiss that gives to it
its sweetness; it is the affection in a kiss that
sanctifies it.

Christian Nestell Bovee

Love is a natural instinct that grows if it is nurtured.
It evolves itself but withers if it is not watered with affection, care, respect and kindness.

Balroop Singh

Affection will burn cheerily when the white flame of love is flickered out.
Affection is a fire that can be fed from day to day and be piled up ever higher as the wintry years draw nigh.

Jerome K. Jerome

Affection is invaluable. I will accept your heart as payment and change your mind.

Amanda Mosher

Chapter 4

Sad Love Quotes Love

I don't try to remember us but when I do, it brings a smile to my lips and a tear to my eye.

Letting go has never been easy, but holding on can be as difficult, for strength is measured not by holding on, but by letting go.

Loving you is what I've learned so easily. Trying to forget you is the last thing I could possibly learn, because I'm deeply in love with you.

For all those years, I thought I had forgotten you, I made myself believe that I don't love you anymore, yet I always end up longing for you every night.

True love takes courage because you put your heart in a perfect position to get torn into a million pieces.

It is better to be with no one than to be with the wrong one.

I don't hate you for not loving me anymore, but I hate myself for still loving you

Love is like the flame of a candle; both can be extinguished in the quickness of one breath.

One-way love is hard to do, but my heart doesn't know how to stop loving you.

Heartbreak brings us immense pain and suffering but in reality, we must realize that it brings us one step closer to the one we are destined to be with.

Time doesn't heal broken hearts, love does. It all started as a beautiful plan, we were in love, cared for each other, but you left me alone.

If loving you would mean heartbreak and endless quarrels, it would be worth it.

My broken heart will heal after a while.
My goal is to see you and not cry, but smile.

God will mend a broken heart if you will give him all the pieces.

I always knew that looking back to the cries would make me laugh but I never knew that looking back to the laughs would make me cry.

Sometimes I feel so lonely in this world, like I don't belong anywhere or with anyone.

I wish I was a kid again, because skinned knees are easier to fix then broken hearts.

When you have loved unconditionally one man and lost that love, it leaves a wound that never heals, a sad and broken heart, a void forever.

I hate him for leaving when I thought he never would but I love him for staying when I was putting him through so much.

If I should die tonight and the reason remains
unknown, tell not the whole world, but the
one I love that I died of a broken heart, not
because he loved me too little but because
I loved him too much.

Sailing across the seas, a fisherman asks me,
'What is the sand scattered for miles made up
of?
Dear Friend O! The broken hearts of a million
lovers on the earth, all shattered, all scattered.

We enjoy warmth because we have been cold.
We appreciate light because we have been in
darkness. By the same token, we can
experience joy because we have known
sadness.

No matter how smart someone is, they'll
never realize what they have, until it is gone.

Sometimes change is what's best, letting your heart break, and learning how to cope.

Every time I see a couple holding hands,
or just plainly sitting together I look away.
It's not that I hate seeing lovers.
But because it reminds me of a question
nobody can answer…Where's mine?

You are the dream I live with; the wish
I made and the name I always whisper in
every prayer.

When you are happy, you enjoy the music.
But, when you are sad you understand the
lyrics.

Living in the past causes you to miss out on the present. Life is too short to let it pass you by.

Now that you have left and forgotten me, I will hold you in my heart and dreams.

Sometimes I wonder if I will ever be happy with myself. I worry that if I can't be happy with myself, then nobody will ever be happy with me, and that just makes me even more paranoid.

There is a distinct, awful pain that comes with loving someone more than they love you.

Just because I let you go, doesn't mean I wanted to.

I don't know if I'm waiting for you to love me, or if I'm waiting for you to realize what you lost.

My biggest fear is that I will become too comfortable with the idea of being lonely for the rest of my life.

The worst feeling is not being lonely, sometimes it is being forgotten by someone you can't forget.

I can feel myself slowly fading from your mind.

It still hurts to see that you're doing completely okay, without me.

Being Ignored, it's the worst feeling ever.

Dear heart, please stop getting involved in everything.
Your job is to pump blood.
That's it.

It all started as a beautiful plan, we were in love, cared for each other, but you left me alone.

I close my eyes and dream of a time when I wasn't all alone.

I'm lonely and you're lovely and I just want to be with you right now even if you don't want to be with me.

Lust feels like love until it's time to make a sacrifice.

It takes a strong heart to love.
It takes a stronger heart to continue to love after it has been hurt.

Did you miss me while you were looking for yourself out there?

You can't write a story together if you're not on the same page.

Let love in through the narrow crack in the
heart.
Let love warm our once cold bitter hearts.
Let love burn our long-lost passion again.
Be my love once again.

When you depart from me sorrow abides, and
happiness takes his leave.

William Shakespeare

It is one thing to be tempted, another thing to
fall.

William Shakespeare

If you and I can't laugh together, we won't
last together.

Loving you was easy; it's living without you that's going to be difficult.

Every time I see you, I try to hide away.
When we meet it seems I can't let go.
Every time you leave the room I feel I'm fading like a flower.

For all these years, I thought I have forgotten you.
I have made myself believe that I don't love you anymore.
Yet I always end up longing for you every night.

Under love's heavy burden do I sink.

William Shakespeare

It pains me to be quiet when my heart wants to speak.

One-way love is hard to do, but my heart doesn't know how to stop loving you.

When you are gone the pieces of my heart are missing you.

Avril Lavigne

You can close your eyes to things you don't want to see, but you can't close your heart to the things you don't want to feel.

My heart never knew loneliness until you
went away. I'm missing you.

Most people want to be the sun that brightens
up your life, but I'd rather be the moon that
shines down on you in your darkest hours.

We let affection, go unspoken,
We let our love go unexpressed.
We can't find words to tell our feelings,
especially to those we love the best.

My heart hurts so much. I have forgotten
what love feels like.
Is this what life is all about, living in pain?

A broken heart is a heart that has felt love.

I wish I was a kid again, because skinned knees are easier to fix than broken hearts.

It is not a lack of love, but a lack of friendship that makes unhappy marriages.

I wish that I could show you, when you are lonely or in darkness, the astonishing light of your own being.

Hafiz

They say love hides behind every corner,
I must be walking in circles.

You can't rush something you want to last
forever.

Every time I see a couple holding hands,
or just plainly sitting together I look away.
It's not that I hate seeing lovers.
But because it reminds me of a question
nobody can answer.
Where's mine?

I was miserable with him,
I am content with you.
His love brought pain,
Your love is true.

The one's that make you cry, never deserve
your tears, and the ones that do deserve them
will never make you cry.

What is the opposite of two?
A lonely me, a lonely you.

Love is like a weapon it can be the only thing
that is keeping you alive in this world or it
can be the thing that will kill you later

I cannot eat, I cannot drink; the pleasures of
youth and love are fled away: there was a
good time once, but now that is gone, and life
is no longer life

Plato

I told my wife the truth. I told her I was seeing a psychiatrist.
Then she told me the truth: that she was seeing a psychiatrist, two plumbers and a bartender.

Rodney Dangerfield

It hurts when you're ignored by the person whose attention is the only thing you want in the world.

How come I'm still ignored after all I've done for you, I gave you my heart because I cared.

Once you feel avoided by someone, never disturb them again.

She told me she cheated on me, and I couldn't
quite put together which hurt worse.
The knife she held in my heart being twisted
and pushed, or the unexpected knife shoved
into my back by my best friend.

I didn't text you just to exercise my fingers,
I was expecting a reply back.

While you're IGNORING her someone else is
BEGGING for her attention.

I'm not heartless, I've just learned how to use
my heart less.

Sometimes it's better to move on than to hold on to a person who doesn't understand you. Sometimes your absence will teach what your presence cannot.

I'm tired of trying, sick of crying, I know I've been smiling, but inside I'm dying.

There is nothing worse than see them together, knowing I will never have him again.

The hardest part about breaking up is letting go of the last piece of your heart.

Every time you cheat on your wife, it destroys a part of her; soon there will be nothing left. I'm sorry when I constantly want to talk to you. When you take long to reply, I get sad. I'm sorry if I say things that might upset you and if I come off as annoying.
I'm sorry if you don't want to talk to me as much as I want to talk to you. I'm sorry if I tell you about my pointless drama when you don't really care. I'm sorry if I come off as being clingy, but it's just me missing you.

It hurts the worst when the person that made you feel so special yesterday, makes you feel so unwanted today.

I am not really cut out to be alone, even though I tried.
The problem is that as much as I can't force you to love me, I can't force myself to stop loving you

Missing you isn't what hurts.
It's knowing that I had you, that's killing me.

You are gone now and I have turned off the
world around me.

Behind my smile is a hurting heart, behind my
laugh I'm falling apart. Look closely at me
and you will see, the girl I am, it isn't me

O love, the beautiful and brief!

Schiller.

We are never so helplessly unhappy as when we lose love.

Sigmund Freud

It all started as a beautiful plan, we were in love, cared for each other, but you left me alone.

Loving the person that doesn't love you isn't wrong; It's just painful.

I realized that I lost my heart to someone who doesn't care, and found it crying in the corner.

Next time your heart speaks, take notes.

It hurts to breathe because every breath
I take proves I can't live without you.

You can close your eyes to things you don't
want to see, but you can't close your heart to
things you don't want to feel.

If you cry because the sun has gone out of
your life, your tears will prevent you from
seeing the stars.

I'm sorry to say so but, sadly it's true that bang-ups and hang-ups can happen to you.

Dr. Seuss

I wish that we could start again and re-write our love story.

If you love me, let me know.
If not, please gently let me go.

Don't cry because it's over, SMILE because it happened.

Dr. Seuss

If you don't value your life start smoking, you'll die ten years early. Or, start drinking to excess every day, you'll die fifteen years early. Or you could love someone who doesn't love you back, you'll die every day.

Think about any attachments that are depleting your emotional reserves. Consider letting them go.

Oprah Winfrey

Had I been in love, I could not have been more wretchedly blind. But vanity, not love, has been my folly.

Jane Austen, Pride and Prejudice

I am no bird; and no net ensnares me; I am a free human being with an independent will, which I now exert to leave you.

Charlotte Brontë

Nothing turns to hate so bitter as what once was love.

Suffering of any kind is a very clear and unmistakable sign that we have abandoned love.

Dan Brulé

Our love is my regret.
Breaking up is just like having the worst nightmare after having the best dream.

And he that shuts out love, in turn shall be shut out from love, and on her threshold, lie howling in outer darkness.

Alfred Tennyson

I don't know where I stand with him. And I don't know what I mean to him. All I know is that every time I think of him, all I want to do is be with him

Boys never realize how much one little thing can hurt a girl.

One of the most difficult tasks in life is removing someone from your heart.

This is the problem with getting attached to someone, when they leave, you just feel lost.

Not all wounds are visible.

You think I have no feelings, and that I can
do without one bit of love or kindness; but
I cannot live so, and you have no pity.

Charlotte Brontë

When you walked away you took my heart
with you. All you left are pain and tears.

I keep myself busy with the things I do.
But every time I pause, I still think of you.
My heart won't let you go, and I need you to
know, I miss you.

Miley Cyrus

Even the most colorful garden appears like
a graveyard without you.

I won't miss you. I will miss who I thought you were.

It's crazy how you can go months or years without talking to someone but they still cross your mind every day.

My silence is just another word for my pain.

Why do I feel so far away from you even though you are sitting right next to me?

I was born again because of your love, but I died of the same reason.

www.ingramcontent.com/pod-product-compliance
Lightning Source LLC
Chambersburg PA
CBHW071409280526
45787CB00001B/497